GONGOOZLER

Joshua Judson is a poet from Nottingham. He is an alumnus of the Mouthy Poets programme, and a member of the Barbican Young Poets community. His work has appeared in such publications as *The North, Magma, Brittle Star, The White Review, The Rialto* and *Butcher's Dog.*

Gongoozler

Published by Bad Betty Press in 2021
www.badbettypress.com

Cover design by Amy Acre

Printed and bound in the United Kingdom

A CIP record of this book is available from the British Library.

ISBN: 978-1-913268-14-5

Supported using public funding by
ARTS COUNCIL ENGLAND

GONGOOZLER

PRESS

What can't be disposed of otherwise –
what can't be broken down – is taken by the river, spat out or lodged
in mud.

– *SAY*, Will Harris

Gongoozler

gongoozler
/ɡɒŋˈɡuːzlə/

noun INFORMAL
noun: **gongoozler**; plural noun: **gongoozlers**

    a watcher of canals, an idle spectator

Origin

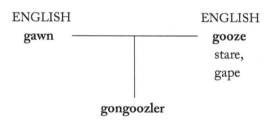

ENGLISH   ENGLISH
  gawn   **gooze**
                                           stare,
                                           gape

                gongoozler

Contents

Gongoozler

Grandma walks down the middle of the road at 3AM.
The tarmac cold under her bare feet, a breeze
coming in off the canal flaring her nightie.

Mist rolling in off the lock.
The trees hold their leaves up
to the yellow glow of the streetlights.

A neighbour fetching a glass of water sees Grandma
from his kitchen window. Puts on slippers.
Walks into the road with an outstretched hand.

Visiting Hours

the dispenser's playing up pretending
like it's got nothing to give but I can see
sanitizer in there under the plastic casing
like an ASDA bag or a yoghurt pot floating
under the frozen surface of the canal
like some old important stolen thing
under glass in a museum but still
the dispenser dry coughs into my hand

I just wanna feel clean I'd cover my whole body
in it if I could sometimes it feels like
my whole body is full of the stuff my insides
cold and acidic I feel brutal stinging
scoured the fucking thing still won't work
but when it does the see-through gel falls
into my palm cold and complete as night
I push the button through to the ward
but I don't feel any better at all

Warm Up

Imagine that you are chewing a piece of gum. Chew it. Focus on the thought of it. You might chew it on one side of your mouth, then the other. Now the gum is expanding. Really work on it. The thought of it. The gum of the thought. Now the gum is made of an idea. Focus on the thought of the gum of the thought. The idea is heavy, it's scratching at the roof of your mouth. It's as if there are feathers in the gum. Crow's feathers. Chew it. Now the gum is made of crow. You might feel a beak complaining against one side of your mouth, then the other. Now the gum is a crow. Focus on the thought of it. There might be blood. The crow might want to screech, and you can let it, just keep chewing. Really work on it. Now the crow is expanding. Your jaw muscles should be good and warm now. Spit out the crow. Think about what you've done.

All I Remember About My Dream Is I Was Happy

and loud in Bodega smoking area. I got on one
of the tables they have out there and shouted
none of you is without sin! waving my glass about.
Taking the piss, presumably. I was wearing nail varnish
that was black as owt which is how I can be sure
it was a dream. One of my weaknesses is cowardice.
I so rarely remember my dreams and when I do,
it's in snatches. I think it was a YouTube video years ago
where I heard that every time you access a memory
you change it. Something about neural pathways but I think
of it as nail varnish chipping away when you use your hands a lot.
Like typing or summat, I wouldn't know. It was my birthday
in the dream I think. Everyone's faces were so bright and happy to see me.

What Work Is

When Mum talks about her dad
she drives her legs apart into the arms of her chair.
She punctuates her sentences with firm drags
on an imaginary Silk Cut. She talks gruff
and low. I swear I've seen her brush ash
from the front of her jumper with his hand.

When Mum talks about my Grandad,
she calls out with his voice to a wife
who is also not here. Says *d'ya want a cuppa, Ruby?*
Says *well get me one while you're up.*

When Mum talks about the man
who wouldn't let her pursue acting,
she becomes him. She re-enacts the scene
where he sends her to catering college in Buxton.
Her face creases, softens. He says
you've got to have a trade.

East Midlands Conference Centre

The setting sun salutes the glass bins.
This mop bucket is our ashtray.
The bar fully stocked, set up
for the delegates who
are due to arrive
any minute.
But for now,
there is
peace.

Gongoozler

The only things rushing in our lives were
the sky sprinting between hills, water thrashing
through the fells in brooks, in gills, in the River Eden.

So when we moved back here, and took the dog
her first walk along the canal, she saw the water
stagnant and repressed in the lock with its carpet of algae.

Mistook it for something solid. The dog crashes into grey.
My forearm dripping. Grabbed by the collar, pulled.
Shaking. Safe.

Poem In Which I Get Out of This Town

Why did the Pop Punk kid cross the road?
To get out of this town.

I've read enough of my fourteen-year-old notebooks
to know that angst alone does not constitute a poetics.
But what if it did? What if that bridge didn't hold me
like a trophy, or an infant, but like she held my bottom lip
between her teeth? There's something more honest about that.
Like there's something more honest about a power chord –
about using just two fingers to play the whole song.
I swear to God I'm getting out of this town.

Sometimes my blood gets so hot. If I can get enough
posters out of Kerrang! Magazine and onto my walls
maybe I'll stop punching them and maybe I'll stop
punching the boys at school, maybe we'll start a band together instead.
One night, the largest of my Green Day posters falls off the wall,
and I wake with a start, their three glossy bodies covering mine.
I swear to God I'm getting out of this town.

It only took me ten years, but I've finally figured it out –
I want to kiss Billie Joe Armstrong from Green Day.
Hold his bottom lip between my teeth like a bridge holds a boy.
If all the memes and the jokes are right, and pop punk
is all just about leaving, then I think all of us listening
were trying to escape the same place. The town of the body.
Where you live is always inadequate, always strange,
only ever beautiful in hindsight.
I swear to God I'm getting out of this town.

If I Acknowledged My Feelings All the Time I'd Never Get Anything Done

and there's buses to catch,
there's coffee to buy and not really want,
there's a whole life to be priced out of.
I can't be thinking of all the people I miss.
There's too many of them to fit in my head
at once and the bus is late and I saw a magpie
and I haven't found his mate yet. Is sorrow
a feeling or just a thing that happens like rain,
or an uncontrollable urge to key cars? Imagine
my surprise to find out I had feelings. Like when you wake
up with blood on your pillow, and then you've got a pillowcase
to soak in cold water. Another thing. I keep grinding my teeth
til I can hear them laughing at me. Thank fuck the bus
is late. I can smoke and scan the sky for magpie wings.
I can smoke and let all the people in my head breathe.
I can smoke until I see the driver. I get on and all my teeth
file on the bus behind me. Laughing still, and pointing now.
Calling me a faggot. And all the people I miss are crushing my head
as if it's stuck between the concertina closing bus doors I didn't ask for any of this

Interior Design

I keep remembering Dad's wedding reception
when Grandpa lost the word *lily*.
My hand out pointing to the centrepiece,
white flowers spilling over onto the table.

I had the garden in my head
when I asked him to name them.
The garden out behind the bungalow he built
that he always kept so neat. I saw him on his knees
in blue overalls, pruning. I saw him pretending
not to mind as a football went crashing
through the fuchsias. Then I saw his eyes,
panicked and dark as the hole where a word should be,
some kind of —

and my dad said *lily* and this is how we manage.
Dad keeps the word *lily*. I keep the sunlight and the grey squirrels
cascading across the lawn on Sunday mornings.
And together we remember everything.

Staffie

I stay close to the ground, clenched.
I love cold days with the dew
on the grass starting to freeze
and a clear sky. I stay close
to the ground with my voice in my pocket.
I'm onside. Every morning I worry
you won't come, that you've gone. In my sleep
I run after you and I whimper.
Don't ever fucking leave me.
I keep your name in my throat
like the ground keeps a seed.
I keep calling you, but we don't speak
the same language.

Stoney Street

I get therapy in Lace Market where the buildings are so tall it makes the sky seem further away I get therapy Sunday mornings so I'm nearly always hungover overthinking the fact of getting therapy somewhere that makes me feel so small Something loud and obnoxious in my headphones to keep me going Something ghostly about the quiet and the halflight Walking past closed up bars that from the outside don't look like they fit in these massive buildings like bars round here are kids dressed in their parents clothes I wait outside in the rain for my therapist to let me into a building designed to display delicate things In therapy I talk about *personal chaos* and *the chaos of other people* bless the white noise of chip paper blowing about outside Lace Market Fish Bar bless every good idea shot down in the offices these buildings are becoming All over Notts you can find these short wide windows like letterboxes taking up almost a whole wall put there to get as much sunlight as possible throughout the day for lace workers I think all the time about looking out on everything from one of those windows I always want to see everything at once but you never can can you

The Night Before Grandpa's Funeral

Mum and I
are in the Co-op in Sandiacre because the one on College St is closed
and we need clotted cream because my grief, tonight, has taken the
form of scones. I could see him snoozing in the living room. I could
see him outside, fixing a fence panel. I needed to do something with
my hands. And I go through to the living room, all flour and butter,
fretting about no cream and I've gotten egg wash on Grandma's Be-Ro
book so we're in the Co-op that Auntie Jean died in front of. Over
the bridge where the hearse stopped for the people who couldn't fit in
the crem, all lined up in anoraks, saying their goodbyes. They've got
clotted cream in big pots and small pots and I get two small ones so
everyone gets a bit of the crust on top and I turn around and Mum has
tomatoes and sourdough and cream cheese and blueberries. All spilling
from her arms, which she will use to comfort the lorry driver next
month in Coroners Court. *It was an accident. She wouldn't have wanted
you to suffer.* And this is probably why I can never leave the shop
with just what I went in for. I'm always trying to feed my grandma's
nine siblings like Mum is. And when we get home my sister and her
boyfriend say their scones are great, and my brother has Nutella on his
like a wrong'un but he gestures to the cooling rack and goes *yeah they're
good them* and tomorrow, when the curtains close around the coffin and
the Nat King Cole song plays I will be the only one not crying.

Ode to Ash

sometimes a while
after I've flicked you
off the end of my fag
part of you will land
on the crook of skin
that joins my thumb
and index finger
having been carried
by the breeze
up in little spirals
and down again
to land on me
and I want to jump up
like our dog Libby
when she was just a puppy
seeing her first snowfall
trying to catch each
slow-falling flake
in her mouth

sometimes part of you
will land in my coffee
and I will drink it anyway
yes sometimes it's raining
and you fall quickly
encased in a drop
of water and make a small
mud pie on the brick
of the front yard

sometimes you collect
in little piles at the foot
of Grandma's chair
or else bruise her small
patch of sky above
Bramcote Crematorium

other times you will land
on my jumper or shirt
which are usually grey already
and when I try to wipe you away
you will hang on
and make a smudge a line
as if I am a charcoal drawing
of myself and you are making space
for the blank page underneath
to represent light hitting me

always though I think
you land where you are
meant to something about
it makes me think of how
an old old song can hit you
exactly where you are
and fill you with light
and I think of Libby
at rest in her box
by the fireplace

Gongoozler

I try to remember my Grandma without the word *dementia*.
I try to walk with her out in the middle of the road, match her for pace.
The leaves on the trees are yellow as in plenty. As in, *real mayonnaise*, not *light*.

Light dappling off the windows of the empty cars,
shining from the thick lenses of her glasses.
I try to match her for pace. Stretch out a hand.

But she turns left down the twitchel to the lock.
She steps out onto the canal and keeps walking.
I can't reach her.

Tombstone

I will come back
as junk at the bottom
of the canal –

bike, shopping trolley, microwave.
You will only be able to see me
on a cold day when the sun is shining

and all the edges
of buildings look sharper
and the detail of the chain link

will be so clear that it will be like the pricking
of the wind against your cheeks.
You will be walking along the towpath.

Your pace will be hurried;
you will pass more magpies than people
and notice

how clear the water of the canal is for once.
How the sun and the cold conspire
to show you something:

how full the canal
has always been,
of just pure stuff.

I will be with you then,
in the spirit of the shape of a bike,
shopping trolley, microwave. Sunk, rusted, gone.

Acknowledgements

This pamphlet is dedicated to the memories of Bill Hickling, Ruby Hickling, and Stuart Judson.

Many thanks are due to everyone who was connected to Mouthy Poets collective which ran for many years out of Nottingham Playhouse, and whose influence is still felt in Nottingham and beyond. Thanks are also due to Jacob Sam-La Rose, Rachel Long and all members of the Barbican Young Poets community which is and has been vital to so many.

Thank you to Chris Lanyon and Laurie Ogden who saw and fed back on earlier versions of this pamphlet.

Thank you to Jake and Amy at Bad Betty for giving the pamphlet a home among an ever-increasing pantheon of amazing poets.

'Warm Up' and an earlier version of 'Ode to Ash' appeared as part of *The White Review*'s online feature for March 2019.

'What Work Is' is after the Philip Levine poem of the same name.

'Interior Design' appeared in Issue 4 of *bath magg*.

An earlier version of 'Stoney Street' appeared in Nottingham's arts and culture magazine *LeftLion* as part of their Snap Notts series, pairing poets with photographers to explore an area of Nottingham.

'Tombstone' appeared in the Barbican Young Poets anthology *An Orchestra of Feathers and Bone*.